The Interest Rate Bootcamp

Thomas Krause

First edition

April 2008

W9-BMH-634

BG Consulting Group Ltd.
7 Harp Lane
London
EC3R 6DP
United Kingdom
www.bgconsulting.com

About the Author

Thomas Christian Krause

Thomas is an experienced professional in the area of capital markets and financial derivatives. He joined BG Consulting Group, a London based provider of high quality, tailored and practical training solutions to the financial service sector, in 2007. Since then, he has trained traders, middle-office, back-office and IT staff from leading investment banks, asset management companies and other financial institutions in Europe and Asia.

He began his career in finance in 1998 in one of the biggest German mortgage banks. As a member of the ALM Team, he managed the bank's interest rate risk in all major currencies for more than six years and specialised in trading interest rate derivatives. In 2000, he started to read economics and business management alongside work and graduated four years later with a diploma in banking and management from the University of Applied Sciences Kaiserslautern.

In late 2005, Thomas was appointed to set up the Derivative Strategies and Trading Team in one of the largest Asset Management companies in Europe. In the process, he introduced several derivative instruments to the company, implemented modern portfolio management concepts and successful overlay trading for both fixed income and equity funds.

After incidentally meeting one of his current colleagues and being taken in by his stories of the glamorous life as a trainer, he joined BG Consulting in March 2007 and specialises in training interest rate, equity and FX derivatives.

Acknowledgements

At this point, I would like to thank everyone who helped me along my path and finally made this book possible. I am greatly indebted to my parents, to my sister and her family and to my favourite granny for their faith, support and understanding. I also must thank my former boss Patrick Ernst for giving up so much spare time to drum the principles of fixed income into my head.

Many thanks to my current employer BG Consulting and to all my friends and colleagues there. In particular, I want to thank Claire Anderson, Richard Class, Russell Hammerson and Sara Beverley for the support, proofreading and many helpful suggestions. The BG graphics team (Claudine Sauvêtre, Hannah Whale and Tom Abbott) did a wonderful job in transforming my scribbling into a professional appearing paperback.

My friends have shown remarkable forbearance and patience during my extensive phase of over commitment and peculiar behaviour. And I hereby promise to a very special girl that one day I will buy the house behind the dyke.

Thomas

Table of Content

1

Interest Rates and Yield Curves

One side effect of a job in banking is that we are showered with jargon words every day. The main reason for creating fancy words in many cases may be the simple desire of the community to sound smart and therefore to justify the high salaries, but we need to be able to "talk the talk" in order to avoid looking stupid – and to tell the truth, some of these words are a genuine help in communicating more precisely. However, if not used correctly, jargon can create misunderstanding and lead to financial losses.

Hence, the first chapter of this book provides an overview about the most important jargon used in connection with interest rate products and will also outline the interpretations used by practitioners. Please be aware that in some cases, our definitions might differ slightly from the ones you have read in textbooks written by people who might have a PhD in finance but have never worked on a trading floor. We do not aim to create confusion, just to reflect reality.

1.1 Rates, Coupons and Yields

Most of the books covering economic topics define interest as the cost of capital – or at least in a very similar way. This explanation sounds civilised and is reasonably short, but it has one problem: it could only be made by economists. For the rest of us, it would be nice to have a less abstract way to justify the existence of interest rates.

Imagine that you are in the comfortable situation of having money you could lend to someone else – wouldn't you want to receive some compensation for temporarily giving up the ability to spend it right now? Or – since most of us are more familiar with the borrower's point of view – if you wanted to use someone else's money for a certain period of time without committing a crime, you would have to pay compensation to the lender. This compensation is called **interest**.

Borrower's point of view	Lender's point of view
Interest is the price the borrower has to pay for the temporary use of someone else's funds.	Interest is the compensation that the lender receives for temporarily giving up the ability to spend money.

From both perspectives, the reason for the existence of interest is that a person has to be paid for temporarily lending money to somebody else. It is therefore correct to interpret interest as the rental fee for money. The percentage of the principal which is paid as a fee over a certain period of time is called the interest rate or coupon rate. The amount that is paid at the end of each period is known as the coupon payment (or just: coupon).

Interest rates are generally quoted as "per annum" rates. That is to say if the coupon is calculated on the basis of a year and is paid once a year in arrears, a one-year investment of €100 at a rate of 4% per annum (p.a.) will pay a return of €4[1] at maturity[2]. Even in the case of an investment period[3] shorter than a year, interest rates are quoted on a per annum basis. This is important

---

[1] In practice, we have to be more precise in calculating this return. An in-depth description of the underlying principles is given in Chapter 2.

[2] The day the lender will get his money back is called the date of maturity.

[3] The investment period describes how long money is surrendered by the lender.

to remember as it means that a three-month investment of €100 at a rate of 4% p.a. won't give you a return of €4 but of around a quarter of €4 (as money is only lent for a quarter of a year). It goes without saying that the coupon is paid at maturity of the investment (i.e. after three months and not after one year).

As there is a huge range of different interest rates in the financial markets (and not just the one risk-free rate that is often mentioned in conjunction with economic models), we need a classification system to be able to describe precisely which rate we are currently talking about. Bodie and Merton[4] introduced a nice approach based on the three main influencing factors of interest rates:

The unit of account

Investments in different currencies pay different interest rates. In other words: the rental fee for money varies depending on the unit in which the payments are denominated. However, a EUR based investor shouldn't just invest his money in GBP denominated bonds with a higher coupon to boost his interest income. Interest rates indeed are currently higher in the UK than in the Euro zone, but investing money in a foreign unit of account always comes with currency risk: the final rate of return depends on future exchange rates between the two currencies.

The maturity

The level of interest rates depends on the period of time until the borrowed amount is repaid. Rates for short-term lending can be higher, lower or equal to rates for long-term lending. In practice, we often plot the relationship between interest rates and the time to maturity in a graph which is then referred to as the yield curve (see: Section 1.2).

---

[4] See: Z. Bodie/R. Merton: "Finance" New Jersey 2000, Prentice-Hall Inc.

Default risk/Credit risk

Lending money generally contains the risk that the borrower won't be able to pay the interest and the principal back in full. The higher the probability of such a default, the higher the rate a lender should charge. The difference between the interest rate of a default risk-free interest rate investment (e.g. a government bond) and an investment that includes a default risk is known as the credit spread.

Another expression that is closely connected with interest rate investments is the yield. The yield of a debt instrument is defined as the annualised percentage increase in the value of the investment. So the question is: what is the difference between a per annum quoted interest rate and a yield?

Well, a bank account that pays an interest of 2% p.a. has also a yield of 2%. But things get slightly more complex if we have a look at bonds. A bond is a debt obligation (similar to a loan) in which the issuer (borrower) promises both to make regular payments of interest and to repay the principal amount to the investor (lender) according to an agreed schedule. The main difference between a loan and a bond is that there is a well-established secondary bond market, especially for government bonds. The investor therefore is able to sell his investment at any time before maturity. But what price will he receive?

Most bonds are issued with a fixed coupon rate which equals the prevailing level of interest rates (market rates) at the time the bond is issued. As interest rates are not stable over time, there could be a divergence between the bond's coupon and market rates. If this is the case, the secondary market price of a bond will decrease if market rates have gone up or increase if market rates have gone down.

If an investor buys a bond with a coupon rate of 4% at a price below 100%, his return will be higher than 4% p.a. as he won't only receive the coupon payments but will also realise capital gains when the bond matures (as the bond is paid back at 100%). The effective interest rate implied by the current market price, maturity and coupon rate of the bond is called the yield of a bond.[5]

As this book is not focussing on bond markets but on interest rates in general, we will use both expressions (interest rates and yields) synonymously from now on.

1.1.1 Yield Curves

As we worked out in Section 1.1, yields in the same currency can differ in two dimensions: maturity and credit risk. In constructing a yield curve[6], we have to make sure that we only use interest rates for investments of a homogenous credit quality, as different issuer sectors have different yield curves. Lower quality sectors should always trade at progressively higher yield levels. In other words, a BBB rated corporate bond should yield higher than a AAA rated government bond.

Practitioners therefore utilise several separate yield curves to reflect the differences in credit quality. One of the most often used curves is called the **risk-free curve**. It is usually constructed from the available series of interest rates on government bonds and, for this reason, considered to be default risk free. The absence of credit risk within securities issued by governments means that government curves have gained benchmark status in all major currencies. In practice, we normally relate interest rates for every credit risk against the relevant risk-free government rate.

---

[5] An introduction to bond pricing is given in Chapter 3. To learn more details about bond pricing, price/yield relationships, etc., see: S. Cowley: "The Best Little Bond Book...Ever!" London 2005, BG Consulting Group Ltd.

[6] The yield curve (also: term structure of interest rates) depicts the yields of investments versus their respective terms to maturity.

Example

Ten-year US government bonds (also called: Treasury bonds) are currently yielding 4.40%. A ten-year A rated corporate bond in USD with a yield of 5.80% is then quoted as Treasuries + 140 basis points.

A yield curve generally can show four basic shapes: **positively sloped**, **inverted** (negatively sloped), **flat** and **humped**:

Figure 1: Positive (or: normal) yield curve

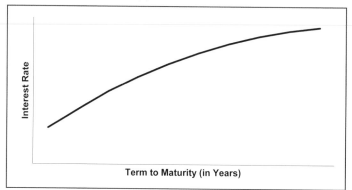

Figure 2: Negative (or: inverted) yield curve

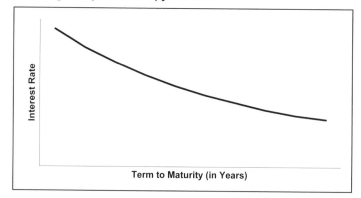

Figure 3: Flat yield curve

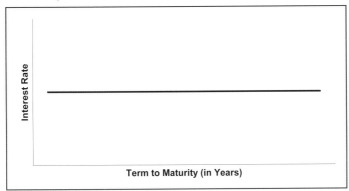

Figure 4: Humped yield curve

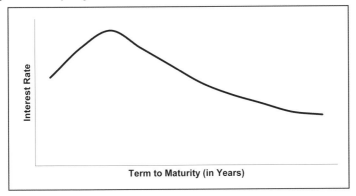

There are many theories trying to explain the different shapes of yield curves, but none of these models work for every interest rate environment. Meanwhile, economists are slowly starting to realise that market mechanics are too complex to squeeze into a single model. So the current trend is to postulate that market developments could only be described by a mixture of those theories.

At least, we can derive some general comments about yield curves and their driving factors from market practice. The principal factor affecting short-term interest rates is the monetary policy executed by the central banks. A restrictive monetary policy leads to higher short-term rates and that often creates a flat or inverted yield curve shape. By contrast, an accommodative monetary policy forces short-term interest rates to lower levels, steepening the yield curve.

The long end of the curve is more influenced by inflation expectations. If inflation fears rise, investors require a higher inflation risk premium for longer term investments. Conversely, as inflation fears subside and investors therefore expect a decline in interest rates, the yield curve flattens or inverts as the demand for long-term investments surges.

Nowadays, the long end of the curve in many currencies (e.g. GBP, EUR) is also influenced by a mismatch between supply and demand in bond markets. The ongoing high demand for long-dated bonds – especially caused by pension funds – is not covered by the current supply. This has pushed up prices of these securities and consequently pushed down their yields.

Exercise

1. Give a brief explanation why a corporate bond yield should be higher than the yield of a government bond with the same maturity. What are the two main factors influencing that spread?

2. Why can two bonds from the same issuer in the same currency and with identical maturities have different credit spreads?

Research Tasks

1. During the last couple of years, "carry trades" have been very popular. Please find an answer to each of the following questions:
    - How could a carry trade be described?
    - What is an essential precondition to a carry trade?
    - Would you describe a carry trade as an arbitrage?
    - What is the main risk in carry trading?

2. Please work out the current shape of the GBP government yield curve and try to interpret it. What does the market expect the Bank of England to do in the future? Which driving factors are currently influencing the longer end of the curve? Check your answers with your colleagues from research.

2

Interest Rate Payments

2.1 Simple Interest Rates

As a general rule, interest rate related products generate at least one interest rate payment during their lifecycle. The generic formula to calculate such a payment looks very simple on first sight:

Equation 1

$$IRP = N * i * DCF$$

where:
IRP	=	Interest rate payment
N	=	Notional amount
i	=	Interest rate (per annum)
DCF	=	Day count fraction

As interest rates could also be referred to as the "rental fee" for money, it makes perfect sense that the amount of interest to pay depends on the notional amount as well as on the interest rate and the coupon period[7]. What makes things slightly more complex in practice is the fact that there is more than one convention used in capital markets to define the exact length of the

---

[7] Generally speaking, interest rates are paid at least once a year. The period of time between two interest rate payments is also referred to as the coupon period. For example, a 1y investment with quarterly coupon payments has a coupon period of three months.

coupon period. In other words: for the same period, we can see different DCF values depending on the financial instrument, the underlying currency and sometimes even the wishes of the client. In other words: from now on, the reader of this book is no longer allowed to answer the question: "if I invest €100 for one year at a rate of 6%, how much interest will I receive?" with a simple "€6". The perfect answer would be: "it depends!"

The DCF is generally defined as the quotient of the number of days within the coupon period and the number of days in the year:

Equation 2

$$DCF = \frac{IRD_{couponperiod}}{IRD_{year}}$$

where: IRD   = Interest rate days

As the number of days should be the same for every financial instrument, why can we get different results for the DCF? Well, the answer is simple: the number of days is not always the same.

In real life, there are of course 30 days between 1st July and the 31st, but in financial markets, this is not necessarily the case. Depending on the investment we are looking at, this coupon period can have 29 or 30 days.

2.1.1 Day Count Conventions

This is quite confusing if you are about to make your first steps in the financial markets. The thing to blame for this mess is called day count convention and it is more or less a body of rules and regulations which:

■   Fixes the way to determine the number of interest days of a coupon period

■   Sets a value for the basis (assumed number of interest rate days per year)

- Gives a description of how to adjust the coupon period and/or the payment day if the last day of the period falls on a holiday or weekend (business day conventions).

Ironically, day count conventions were primarily developed to ease the calculation of interest rate payments. Well, obviously that was before computers were invented, so we missed that benefit and all that's left for us is another needless complication of our daily lives.

A day count convention generally consists of three parts. The first part assesses the way to determine the number of interest days within the given coupon period. In practice, we can find three different, widespread methods to do this:

ACT	This method considers the actual number of days, including weekends and bank holidays but excluding the period's starting day.	01/03-31/03: 30 days 01/03-01/04: 31 days
30E	All months are assumed to have 30 days, resulting in a 360-day year. If the starting date falls on a 31st, it is changed to the 30th. If the end date falls on a 31st, it is also changed to the 30th. The starting day is excluded in the counting.	01/03-31/03: 29 days 31/03-30/04: 30 days
30	All months are assumed to have 30 days, resulting in a 360-day year. If the starting date falls on the 31st, it's changed to the 30th. If the end date falls on the 31st, it is also changed to the 30th, but only if the first date falls on the 30th or 31st. The starting day is excluded in the counting.	01/03-31/03: 30 days 31/03-30/04: 30 days

Counting interest days using the methods 30E and 30 for longer periods manually could be annoying. How fortunate that we can simplify the calculation using the following formula:

Equation 3

$$IRD_{period} = (y_2 - y_1) * 360 + (m_2 - m_1) * 30 + (d_2 - d_1)$$

where: y_2 = Year of maturity day (YYYY)

y_1 = Year of starting day (YYYY)

m_2 = Month of maturity day (MM)

m_1 = Month of starting day (MM)

d_2 = Maturity day (DD)

d_1 = Starting day (DD)

Adjustment rules:

30:    d_1: $31 \rightarrow 30$

d_2: $31 \rightarrow 30$, only if d_1 is 30 or 31

30E: d_1: $31 \rightarrow 30$

d_2: $31 \rightarrow 30$

The second part of the day count convention determines how many days per year are assumed. And again, we can find three different modes used on the financial markets:

ACT	Leap year counts for 366 days, non-leap year counts for 365 days.
360	A year is assumed to have 12 months of 30 days each.
365	All years are assumed to have 365 days.

The last part of the day count convention defines the procedure used for adjusting the end date of a coupon period or just the payment day in response to days that are not business days. The most common conventions are:

Adjusted, modified following	Payments that fall on a holiday or weekend roll forward to the next good business day, unless that day falls in the next calendar month, in which case the payment day rolls back to the preceding business day. The coupon period is adjusted.
	Example: if the period spans from 30th June to 30th September and 30th September is a Sunday, the payment is made on Friday, 28th, as the next good business day following the 30th September (Monday, 1st October) will be in the next calendar month. The coupon period will be adjusted so that we only have to pay interest for the days between 30th June and 28th September.
Unadjusted following	Payments that fall on a holiday or a weekend roll forward to the next business day. The coupon period won't be adjusted, so the interest payment will be made for the days between 30th of June and 30th of September on Monday, 1st October.
Adjusted preceding	Payments that fall on a holiday or weekend roll back to the preceding business day.

People often tend to underestimate the essential role of day count conventions in the fixed income world at the beginning of their careers. But this is only temporary: after they have lost a couple of thousand dollars in a single trade because they didn't care about day count conventions, most of them stop being so careless. To prevent you from encountering this unpleasant situation, let's make sure that you will never forget the power of day count conventions.

Here are the different interest rate payments for the same period (1st May-31st May, leap year, 31st is a business day) and the same rate (5% p.a.) on an amount of €100,000,000 using several day count conventions:

Day count convention	IRD$_{period}$	Basis	Payment
ACT/360	30	360	416,666.67
30/360	30	360	416,666.67
30E/360	29	360	402,777,78
ACT/365	30	365	410,958.90
ACT/ACT	30	366	409,836.07

As you can see, the payment can differ quite considerably. And if you are not currently sitting either in a cabin full of respectable looking professionals or in an annual strategy meeting with your line manager, it's definitely a good time to shout the following sentence at least three times: **It is never enough to base an investment decision just on the given interest rate!**

Now as we know this, we are allowed to ignore day count conventions in the following chapters for simplification – but of course, you will never do this in practice.

2.1.2 The Equivalent Rate

If you want to compare fixed income investments with different day count conventions directly, you have to calculate the so-called equivalent rate. The idea of this process is to transform the interest rate given for a certain day count convention into an interest rate for the day count convention the initial rate should be compared with.

Let's assume we want to invest 1,000,000 for a period of one month (1st May-31st May, no leap year, 31st is a business day) and ask two banks for bids. Bank A quotes 3.97% on an ACT/360 basis, Bank B is willing to pay 4.01% but on an ACT/365 basis. Which investment alternative should we choose? To find the answer, we can calculate the equivalent ACT/360 rate for the 4.01% offer on an ACT/365 basis. This could be done using the following formula:

Equation 4

$$i_e = i_g * DCF_g / DCF_t$$

where:
	i_e	= Equivalent rate
	i_g	= Rate for given day count convention
	DCF_g	= Day count fraction for given day count convention
	DCF_t	= Day count fraction for target day count convention

For our example, we will have to calculate:

$$i_e = 4.01\% * \frac{30}{365} * \frac{360}{30} = 3.9551\%$$

The equivalent ACT/360 rate for the 4.01% alternative would only be 3.9551%. This is roughly 1.5 basis points (1 basis point = 0.01%) lower than the 3.97% offered by the Bank A. So even if the 4.01% looks much more attractive on first sight, we should go for the 3.97% as the return in terms of real money will be higher.

Alternative A

$$\text{Return} = 1{,}000{,}000 * 3.97\% * \frac{30}{360} = 3{,}308.33$$

Alternative B

$$\text{Return} = 1{,}000{,}000 * 4.01\% * \frac{30}{365} = 3{,}295.89$$

2.2 Appendix

The current standard conventions for the different segments of major financial markets:

Currency	Money Market	Bond Markets	Swaps
EUR	ACT/360	Annual ACT/ACT	Annual 30E/360 vs. 6M EURIBOR
GBP	ACT/365	Semi-annual ACT/ACT	Semi-annual ACT/365 vs. 6M LIBOR
USD	ACT/360	Semi-annual ACT/ACT	Semi-annual 30/360 vs. 3M LIBOR
JPY	ACT/360	Semi-annual ACT/365	Semi-annual ACT/365 vs. 6M LIBOR
CHF	ACT/360	Annual 30E/360	Annual 30E/360 vs. 6M LIBOR

Exercises

1. Please calculate the interest payments for the following investments:

1	Start date:	18.11.2007
	Maturity:	03.12.2007
	Interest rate:	5%
	Notional:	100 million
	Day count:	ACT/360

2	Start date:	01.03.2006
	Maturity:	31.01.2007
	Interest rate:	4.5%
	Notional:	100 million
	Day count:	30/360

3	Start date:	01.02.2008
	Maturity:	03.03.2008
	Interest rate:	4%
	Notional:	100 million
	Day count:	ACT/ACT

2. Please calculate the equivalent ACT/360 rates for Investment 2 and 3.

3. Please have another look at Alternative 2. Assuming that the 31.01.2007 is a Sunday, which information do we need to calculate the resulting interest payment?

Time Value of Money and Bond Pricing

3.1 Compound Interest and Future Value

Whenever the investment period[8] contains more than one coupon payment, the return is not that easy to calculate. Granted, we can still calculate the individual coupon payments, but simply adding them up and then using the sum to compare two investment alternatives might be convenient but inaccurate.

In all likelihood, the investor will reinvest the periodic coupon cash flows for the remaining time (or at least, he might do it). That is to say that in the case of a multi-coupon-period investment, interest is earned on both the principal amount and on the coupon receipts. This interest-on-interest component differentiates compound interest from simple interest.

Figure 5 clarifies this difference for a 10y investment of 100 with a coupon of 4% (day count ignored for simplicity). The total sum of all coupon payments is 40, presuming a reinvestment rate for all coupons of 4% the return is boosted by another 8.02 of interest on interest:

---

[8] In contrast to the coupon period, the investment period describes the entire duration of the investment and not only the period of time between two coupon payments.

Figure 5

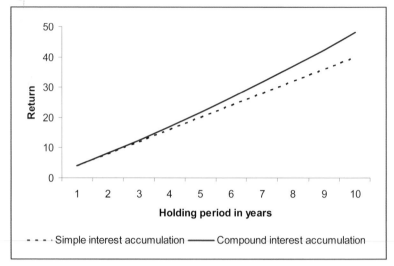

But how can we calculate this compounding effect? Well, under the assumption that the reinvestment rate is stable for the whole duration of the investment, this is not very difficult.

Let's think about a two-year credit risk-free investment with an annual coupon of 4% (day count ignored for simplicity). If we invest 100, we will receive a coupon payment of 4 after Year 1. This coupon is reinvested for the remaining year also at a rate of 4% so that the total coupon payment after Year 2 won't be 4 but (100 * 4%) + (4 * 4%) = 4.16. As the lump sum of the two investments (the initial investment of 100 and the reinvestment of 4) will also be paid back after Year 2, the total return for a two-year investment at a rate of 4% will be 8.16. These cash flows are illustrated in Figure 6:

Figure 6

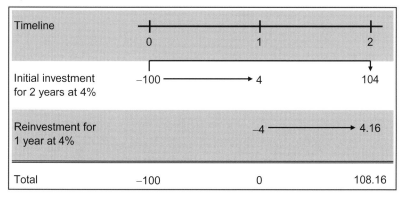

This result could also be worked out mathematically:

$$\text{Total payback} = \left[100 * (1 + 4\%)\right] * (1 + 4\%) = 100 * (1 + 4\%)^2 = 108.16$$

By the end of Year 2, the investment has grown to a value of 108.16. This amount is also referred to as the investment's future value[9].

In general, the future value of an investment for **n** periods with an interest rate **i** per period can be calculated using the following formula:

Equation 5

$$FV = PV * (1 + i\%)^n$$

where: FV   = Future value of an investment (its value at the future time period n)

PV   = Present value (the investment amount)

i   = The period rate (if n is in years, it's the per annum rate, if n is in quarters, it's a quarter of the annual rate, etc.)

n   = Number of periods over which interest is received and reinvested

---

[9] In this context the investment amount of 100 is denoted by the present value.

This formula makes it very easy to calculate the future value of a multi-period interest rate investment. Unfortunately, the fundamental assumption (every coupon payment could be reinvested at the same rate) is a little bit removed from reality. The following chart shows the variation of two-year risk-free interest rates in EUR over just three months in late 2007:

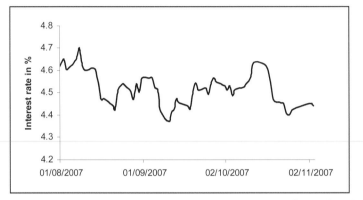

Source: Bloomberg

As we can see, interest rates are anything but stable in practice. It is highly unlikely that on the day of the coupon payment, interest rates will be at the same level as on the inception day of the investment.

Even if interest rates were unchanged when the first coupon is paid, the reinvestment assumption would still lead to a falsified result for the majority of scenarios. The reason for that is that we also have to take the term structure of interest rates (i.e. the shape of the yield curve) into account.

As we have learned in Chapter 1, the interest rate for different maturities is usually not identical – we can see upward sloping (normal), downward sloping (inverted) or humped yield curves (with both normal and inverted parts). The following table shows a EUR government yield curve:

Maturity in years	Interest rate
1	3.98%
2	4.00%
3	4.07%
4	4.11%
5	4.12%

Let's go back to our two-year 4% investment and assume that at the day of the first coupon payment, interest rates are still exactly where they were one year ago. As the remaining investment period is only one year, the reinvestment rate will be 3.98% and not 4%. The future value will consequently be lower than calculated using Equation 5.

So why did we waste a couple of pages discussing an approach to calculate the future value of an investment, when the result won't be correct in most cases? The answer is simple enough: market practice ignores these worries and uses the principles of Equation 5 for pricing purposes. Some say, this is because the market participants are too lazy to learn a new, more accurate method or that this simplification is essential for a fully functional market. All we know is that's how the bond market works.

3.2 Bond Pricing

A fixed rate bond is a debt security, in which the issuer owes the holder a debt and is obliged to make fixed regular interest payments (the coupon) and to repay the principal at maturity. A bond therefore is quite similar to a loan. The main difference is that there is a liquid secondary market for bonds: i.e. in most cases, it is comparatively easy and cheap to sell a bond before maturity.

The interest rate the issuer has to pay depends on a number of different factors. We have already identified the main factors in Chapter 1:

1. The unit of account (i.e. the set of risk-free rates for the underlying currency)

2. The maturity

3. The issuer and maturity specific credit risk

Let's work out the concept of bond pricing using the following example. A European government[10] wants to issue a 5y bond in EUR. As the credit spread for a government bond is zero by definition[11], the required yield is 4.12%. In our example, the bond is issued with a fixed annual coupon of 4.12% and we buy 100 million notional in the morning. The notional amount of a financial instrument is the nominal or face amount used to calculate the interest payments (see Equation 1). In bond markets, it also represents the amount paid back by the issuer at maturity. Later that day, the European Central Bank cuts its key interest rate unexpectedly by 0.5%. This move has a significant impact on interest rates in general so that the EUR government bond curve looks very different in the early afternoon[12]:

Maturity in years	Interest rate
1	3.23%
2	3.25%
3	3.27%
4	3.32%
5	3.35%

[10] For simplification, we are assuming that the inherent credit risk is identical for every government in the Euro area, so we do not have to specify the government further.

[11] See Section 1.2

[12] Although interest rates were only cut by 50bp, yields have gone down much further. Such an exaggerated move can often be observed if something completely unexpected happens in financial markets, and expectations of further interest rate cuts are now factored into yields.

We now decide that we want to invest our cash (100 million) in the stock market because we expect to receive a better return than the fixed 4.12% per annum over the next few months. So we must look to sell this bond to another investor.

Fortunately, our timing was perfect. We invested our €100 million in the morning for five years at a rate of 4.12% per annum whereas an investor who invests cash in that bond right now would only receive 3.35% (current five-year government rate). As we do not want to be the only market participant who might dispense lunch for free, we won't sell the bond to another investor without receiving some reward for having got the market right. This reward will be realised by selling the bond for a higher price than the purchase price.

Bond prices are generally quoted as a percentage rate of the notional amount and one can say that the bond price fulfils the role of adjusting the fixed coupon of a bond to the current level of interest rates. In our example, we invested money for five years at the then-current market rate of 4.12%. As the coupon was also fixed at this level, there was no need for adjustment, so we had to pay a price of 100% (the initial payable amount was €100 million). After the landslide in interest rates, the bond will still pay a fixed coupon of 4.12%. However, we have already stated that an investor buying the bond at current interest rates can only expect to receive a return of 3.35% for his investment. As bonds are usually redeemed at a price of 100%, the investor therefore has to pay a price of above par, and this overpayment will have the effect of reducing payments of 4.12% to a total return level of 3.35%. But how do we calculate the exact price?

3.2.1 The Time Value of Money

The main conclusion of this concept is that two payments (or more generally: cash flows) of the same amount will not have the same value for the receiver when they take place in different points in time. In practice, we all should prefer to receive €1 million today than in one year's time.

This concept is very widespread in financial markets and consists of two building blocks: the future value and the present value. We have already discussed the future value at the beginning of this chapter and condensed the results in Equation 5:

$$FV = PV * (1 + i\%)^n$$

However, in financial markets, we often want to identify the present value of a future cash flow, i.e. how much a certain payment at a given date in the future is worth today. This process is called **discounting**.

In this case, we know the future value of the investment. If we also know the relevant interest rate and the number of investment periods, we can easily rearrange Equation 5 to solve it for the PV:

Equation 6

$$PV = \frac{FV}{(1 + i\%)^n}$$

Mathematically, this is very easy to do but it may be a bit abstract. So what does the present value really represent?

Let us assume we know that we will receive a payment of €1 million in one year's time. This payment is guaranteed and we can be sure that we will receive it. Certainly a nice situation to be in but for those among us who are impatient, it would be nicer if the money could be spent today. There is an easy way to achieve this: we can simply sell the cash flow for the current present value. Acknowledged, we won't receive the full €1 million but at least we can go shopping straight away. But how can we sell a future cash flow? Well, as a private person, this could easily be done in taking out a one-year loan. All we have to do is to adjust the loan amount so that the total payment at maturity will be €1 million. If the interest rate we have to pay for the loan is 3.98%, we can say that 103.98% of the loan amount should equal €1 million:

$$103.98\% = 1{,}000{,}000$$

So:

$$100\% = \frac{1{,}000{,}000}{1.0398} = 961{,}723.41$$

The loan amount in this case is €961,723.41 and the interest that has to be paid for the year is going to be €38,276.59 (€961,723.41 * 3.98%). The total loan expenses of €1 million after one year could be met with the initial receivable so that we can conclude: the present value of €1 million to be received in one year with one-year rates at 3.98% p.a. is €961,723.41.

Using Equation 6, we will receive the same result:

$$PV = \frac{FV}{(1 + i\%)^n} = \frac{1{,}000{,}000}{(1 + 3.98\%)^1} = 961{,}723.41$$

To show how the formula can be extended for periods greater than one year, let's calculate the present value of a payment of €1 million to be received in two years from now, with two-year rates at 4%:

$$PV = \frac{FV}{(1 + i\%)^n} = \frac{1{,}000{,}000}{(1 + 4\%)^2} = 924{,}556.21$$

3.2.2 The Bond Pricing Formula

But how can this concept be applied to calculate the price of our five-year government bond? Technically, a bond is nothing else than a series of cash flows: periodic interest payments predefined by the fixed coupon and the notional or face value that is payable at maturity. For our five-year bond with a coupon of 4.12%, we can roll out the following cash flows:

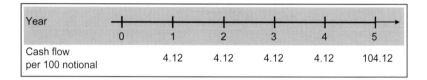

Year	0	1	2	3	4	5
Cash flow per 100 notional		4.12	4.12	4.12	4.12	104.12

The fair price of a fixed bond equals the present value of the stream of cash flows the bond generates. In other words: to calculate the bond price, we just have to discount the single cash flows back to today and sum up the corresponding present values. Formula-wise, the bond price function could be outlined as follows:

Equation 7

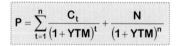

$$P = \sum_{t=1}^{n} \frac{C_t}{(1+YTM)^t} + \frac{N}{(1+YTM)^n}$$

where:
n = Maturity of the bond (in years)
C_t = Coupon at Time t
N = Face value
YTM = Yield to maturity

The yield to maturity is the current market rate for a bond with the given features. In our case, the required yield was 4.12% the moment the bond was issued. If we apply this rate to Equation 7, we will get the following result:

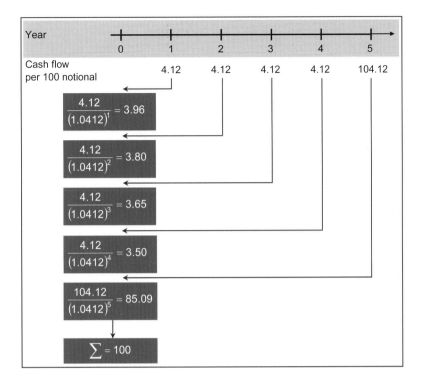

The bond price at issuance therefore has to be at 100%, which is not surprising as we defined the bond price as mechanism to adjust the fixed coupon to the current market interest rate. If both rates are the same, there is no adjustment and the bond price by definition is at 100.

Let's repeat the calculation using the lower interest rates which were observable after the rate cut: five-year risk-free rates have gone down to 3.35%. The stream of cash flows from the bond has not changed, as the coupon is fixed for the whole term of the bond. So we only have to repeat the above calculation using the new yield to maturity of 3.35%. The new market price should be at:

$$P = \frac{4.12}{(1.0335)^1} + \frac{4.12}{(1.0335)^2} + \frac{4.12}{(1.0335)^3} + \frac{4.12}{(1.0335)^4} + \frac{104.12}{(1.0335)^5} = 103.49$$

Since this calculation requires a lot of inputting into a calculator, there are all too many chances of making mistakes. It therefore always makes sense to run a little plausibility check to see if the result makes sense. We know from Equation 7 that there is an inverse relationship between the bond price and the yield to maturity, i.e. if the yield goes up the bond price goes down and vice versa. As interest rates in our example have gone down, the bond price should have gone up so that a bond price above 100 makes sense. But that would also be the case if we calculate a bond price of let's say 106.33. So the second step is to make sure that the price difference (Δprice) is plausible. We know that after we bought the bond, interest rates have gone down from 4.12% to 3.35%. So we will receive an interest rate which is 0.77% (4.12% – 3.35%) above the current market rate for the next five years. Due to the fact that payments in the future have to be discounted to calculate their present value, we can definitely say that the price change (Δprice) cannot exceed 3.85% (5 * 0.77%). So any bond price above 103.85% must be wrong as long as there are positive market rates, which normally is the case.

As we have seen, bond pricing is relatively easy and straightforward. But as we have already learned at the beginning of this chapter, the underlying assumptions can be very far removed from reality. The formula will only lead to a correct result under the following assumptions:

1. A perfectly flat yield curve with market rates for all maturities at the level of the yield to maturity (all payments are discounted using the same interest rate no matter at which point in time they will occur)

2. Reinvestments over the whole life of the bond could be made at a constant rate equalling the yield to maturity (discounting with the formula $x/(1+YTM)^t$ automatically assumes that the interim coupon payments could be reinvested at the same rate)[13]

---

[13] To recap, please refer back to section 3.1

But doesn't that mean that bond prices are wrong? Well, the bond price formula is based on assumptions which hardly ever reflect absolute reality but as bonds are trading at these prices, it would not be right to say that they are wrong – the market price is where the market is currently trading. In practice, bonds are quoted on a price basis anyway so that we don't have to apply the formula for pricing purposes. However, the formula is used to calculate the implied yield to maturity from a given bond price and that approach is problematical: the final yield of a bond investment does not only depend on coupon and purchase price but also on the reinvestment rates that are achieved for the interim coupon payments. So to conclude: the bond price itself is right but the derived implied yield will only be realised under the unlikely assumption that reinvestment of all interim coupon payments could be made at the level of the yield to maturity. In conclusion, reinvestment risk is ignored for the purposes of bond pricing.

3.3 Reinvestment Risk

In reality, we cannot say with certainty where interest rates will be in the future or how the shape of the curve will look, so we don't know at which rate the interim coupon payments could be reinvested. Consequently, we can't derive precisely the final yield of the bond investment – this uncertainty is often referred to as reinvestment risk.

If interest rates go up – or just stay stable in case of an inverted curve – the reinvestment rate for the received coupon payments will be higher. The simplified formula (Equation 5) will therefore underestimate the effect of compounding. On the other hand, the effect will be overestimated if rates go down – or interest rates stay stable in case of a normal yield curve.

To clarify reinvestment risk, the following figure shows us the future value of our two-year 4% investment (we have already seen this in Section 3.1) but this time under the assumption that the coupon payment after Year 1 could only be reinvested at a rate of 3% because interest rates have fallen dramatically:

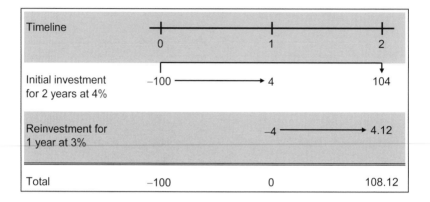

As you can see, the total return is now 108.12 at maturity rather than 108.16 under the assumption of a reinvestment rate of 4%. Whilst this difference of 0.04 may seem trivial, every cent counts in the financial markets. Moreover, the investment shortfall would become far more pronounced for a longer term investment.

With the reinvestment risk in mind, it is useful to compare two investment alternatives with the same maturity but with different coupon payment dates and/or different coupon periods. To make the alternatives comparable, we first have to eliminate the reinvestment risk using more sophisticated financial products. How this can be done will be discussed in the following chapter.

Exercises

1. Please calculate the future value of a seven-year investment of €500 at a rate of 4% per annum and semi-annual payments.

2. Please discount €1,000 to be received in ten years back to today using the current ten-year rate of 4.20%. Assume this rate is paid annually.

3. Last year, a company issued a four-year bond with an annual coupon of 4% and redemption at par. If the bond now has three years until maturity and yields 4.5%, what is the price of the bond?

4. Bellring Inc., an American telephone company, issued a four-year bond two years ago (coupon 7%). At that time, they were rated B+. In the last few years, the management has done a very good job and Bellring was upgraded to BBB– last week. Consequently, the credit spread against US Treasuries for this bond narrowed down to 25bp. Two-year Treasury yields are currently trading at 5.03%. What is the price for Bellring's bond today?

4

Types of Interest Rates

4.1 Coupon Rates

Until now we have only discussed coupon rates (also known as par rates) and we have already realised that it requires more than just a simple comparison of particular interest rates if you want to identify the best investment alternative.

Along with the day count convention, a par rate defines the amount of interest that is paid on a fixed income investment at the end of every coupon period. The coupon is expressed as a percentage of the principal (also referred to as the face value) and is paid regularly (e.g. annually, monthly, etc.).

4.2 Zero Rates

At the end of Chapter 3, we brought up a phenomenon called reinvestment risk. We worked out that every investment paying a fixed coupon generates a predictable cash flow, but as we do not know at which rate the single coupon payments can be reinvested for the remaining investment horizon, we are not able to calculate the precise final total return at this stage. All we can say is that the final return of every coupon paying investment depends, to a certain extend, on the future development of interest rates.

But how about investors who are looking for a fixed income investment without any reinvestment risk? Is there no multi-period fixed income instrument which will meet those needs? The good news: there is and it's called a zero-coupon investment (often also referred to as a zero-coupon bond or just "zero bond").

The idea is simple: as the reinvestment risk is caused by the interim coupon payments between start date and maturity of the investment, there is no coupon paid for the investment – that will automatically eliminate all reinvestment risk. But who would invest his money when he will not receive compensation for temporarily giving up the power of disposal? As the answer should be "nobody", a zero bond must offer another form of compensation mechanism than regular coupon payments – otherwise, it would simply not exist. And indeed, a zero bond employs the use of a discount price, i.e. a zero-coupon investment entails the exchange of a cash flow today for a larger cash flow at maturity.

In order to compare two different zero-coupon investments, we might want to calculate an implied annualised interest rate for a zero-coupon investment. Let's say that we would rather buy a 5y government zero bond instead of investing our €100 million in a 5y coupon bond like we have done in Chapter 3. The purchase price of that bond is 81.701% and there will be a payment of 100% at maturity, i.e. in five years. So the cash flow stream consists only of two payments: the payment of the purchased price at t_0 and the final payment at t_5:

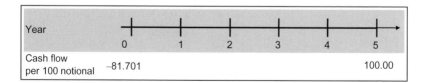

The EUR government yield curve is again given as follows:

Maturity in years	Coupon rate
1	3.98%
2	4.00%
3	4.07%
4	4.11%
5	4.12%

To calculate the implied annualised yield of that investment, we have to refer back to Equation 5. We already know the present value (81.701%) and the future value of our investment (100%), but we are looking for the implied interest rate. So we have to rearrange the formula and solve it for the interest rate this time:

$$FV = PV * (1 + i\%)^n \Rightarrow \frac{FV}{PV} = (1 + i\%)^n$$

$$\Rightarrow \sqrt[n]{\frac{FV}{PV}} - 1 = i\%$$

$$\Rightarrow \sqrt[5]{\frac{100}{81.701}} - 1 = 4.125\%$$

Why do we use the standard formula for future value calculation although we know that the underlying assumption is wrong?

Well, we use this formula because this time it is right to use it. Remember, the main point of critique was that the formula does not take the reinvestment risk into account. It is based on the simple assumption that interim coupon payments could always be reinvested at the same interest rate (i). But in the present case, this constraint is of no consequence, as there are no interim coupon payments in a zero-coupon investment. That is to say, it is correct to use Equation 5 to calculate the future value, present value or implied annualised rate for any zero-coupon instruments. For this reason, we want to adjust this formula slightly:

Equation 8

$$FV = PV * (1 + z_n)^n$$

where: z_n = zero rate for n-years

Why is the implied zero yield 4.125% 0.5 basis points[14] higher than the normal five-year EUR government rate of 4.12%?

The main difference between a five-year government coupon bond and the present zero bond is that there are no cash flows between the purchase date and the maturity of the zero bond, whereas the coupon bond entails a regular income stream in the form of an annual coupon. The lack of interim coupon payments leads to the fact that a zero bond is literally reinvestment risk free. On the one hand, this could be interpreted as an advantage, as we can easily calculate the total return of our investment at t_0 and the investor does not have any exposure to future changes of interest rates. On the other hand, buying a zero bond not only eliminates the reinvestment risk but also the possibility to achieve any reinvestment returns. The holder of a coupon bond can reinvest the interim coupon payments and as long as interest rates are positive, this will give him an extra income (interest on interest or compound interest[15]). To compensate the investor in a zero bond for this disadvantage, the implied annualised interest rate is often slightly above the coupon bond rate for the same maturity[16].

---

[14] One basis point equals 0.01%.

[15] See Chapter 3.

[16] This is very often the case but can't be generalised. As we will see later, the direction of deviation finally is a result of the yield curve shape, i.e. the market expectations regarding the future development of interest rates.

In practice, the implied annualised yield of a zero-coupon investment is simply called the zero rate and as we have seen, there is a close relationship between coupon and zero rates: a zero rate is the par interest rate for the same maturity with the reinvestment risk removed.

4.2.1 Bootstrapping

The main lesson of the previous section is the fact that the use of Equation 5 leads to correct results as long as we use zero rates. This eliminates the coupon effect and as a result, the discounting of cash flows no longer involves any problematic reinvestment assumptions. In addition, we can use a payment date specific zero rate for every single cash flow so that we do not have to assume a perfectly flat yield curve. Bearing that in mind, the correct approach in pricing our five-year government bond with an annual coupon of 4.12% would be:

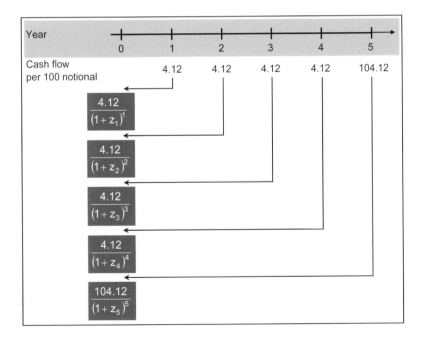

From a technical point of view, this approach does not seem to be too difficult. The problem is that the only observable interest rates in the markets are coupon rates. Zero bonds, which could be used to derive zero rates in an easy way, are only traded very infrequently. So before we can calculate the real present value of the stream of cash flow, we first have to calculate the required zero rates from the given coupon curve.[17] A method often used in practice is referred to as "bootstrapping". This is an iterative approach that calculates zero rates from a given coupon rate curve by eliminating the reinvestment risk for the successive points in time.

Let's clarify this approach using a concrete example. We know, that Equation 8 can be rearranged and solved for the zero rate. In other words: if we know the present value and the future value of a cash flow, we can easily calculate the implied zero rate as follows:

Equation 9

$$\sqrt[n]{\frac{FV}{PV}} - 1 = z_n$$

But how can we calculate the correct present value for a cash flow that will be received in the future? As already said, the only available set of interest rates is a coupon rate curve, as these rates are traded and quoted directly on financial markets. So we have to find a way to use the given coupon rates to calculate the correct present value.

---

[17] This is possible because of the relationship between coupon and zero rates we worked out in Section 4.1: zero rates are coupon rates with the reinvestment risk removed.

Maturity in years	Coupon rate
1	3.98%
2	4.00%
3	4.07%
4	4.11%
5	4.12%

The good news is that the first zero rate is already known. A one-year coupon rate investment with an annual coupon is effectively a one-year zero-coupon investment, as there are no interim coupon payments which will cause reinvestment risk. And whenever the risk profile of two different investment alternatives is identical, the return of these two alternatives must be exactly the same. If this is not the case, the alternative with the higher return will be preferred by the market and the excess demand for this alternative will lead to an increase in its price which will make it less attractive. This automatic market reaction will end as soon as the returns for both alternatives are equal[18]. That is to say, a one-year zero bond and a one-year coupon bond with annual coupon payments must give the same return to the investor: the one-year coupon rate equals the one-year zero rate.

But how can we calculate the zero rates for the subsequent maturities? To explain this we have to go back to the less abstract definition of the present value that was derived in Section 3.2.1. We said there that the present value could be interpreted as the amount we can take out as a loan today when both interim coupon payments and the final redemption payment should be completely financed by the future cash flow. Let's use this concept to calculate the present value of a cash flow of €100 to be received in two years.

---

[18] This principle is well known as the no-arbitrage principle. It's a simple conclusion but this idea is the underlying assumption of nearly all pricing concepts in financial markets. So: never forget!

The first step is to calculate the loan amount that will cause a total final payment (coupon plus redemption payment) of €100 in two years' time. The two-year coupon rate is at 4.00%, so we can say that €100 should be 104% of the loan amount. The loan amount could therefore be calculated as follows:

$$\frac{100}{104\%} = \frac{100}{1.04} = 96.15$$

In other words: if we borrow €96.15 for two years today at the two-year coupon rate of 4%, we have to pay €100 (€3.85 interest and €96.15 redemption payments) at t_2. But as the two-year rate at hand is a coupon rate, we not only have to pay interest for the loan at t_2 but also at t_1 and that complicates our aim to finance all interim payments and the redemption with the future cash flow. So we have to find a way to neutralise the interim cash flow. A simple way to do this is to take part of the borrowed amount in t_0 and invest it for one year. As the return on this investment will be defined by the current one-year rate, we can calculate the amount to be invested as follows:

$$\frac{3.85}{103.98\%} = \frac{3.85}{1.0398} = 3.70$$

If we invest €3.70 at t_0 for one year at a rate of 3.98%, we will receive €3.85 in t_1 from this investment – the lump sum of €3.70 plus the interest of €0.15 (3.70 * 3.98%). This cash flow is then used to offset the coupon payment we have to make for the 2y loan and therefore neutralise the interim cash flow. But it will also reduce the initial available amount. Hence, the real present value for the cash flow to be received at t_2 could be calculated via a simple subtraction: 96.15 – 3.70 = 92.45. The following diagram clarifies the applied principles:

Timeline	0	1	2
Known cash flow in 2 years			100
Cash flow of a 2y loan (€96.15) at a rate of 4% annual coupon	96.15	coupon: $-96.15*4.00\%$ $= -3.85$	final payment: $-96.15 + (-3.85)$ $= -100$
Cash flow of a 1y investment (€3.70) at 3.98%, annual coupon	-3.70	final payment: $3.70 + (3.70*3.98\%)$ $=3.85$	
Total	92.45	0	0

Now, as we know the future value and the present value, we can calculate the implied zero rate:

$$\sqrt[2]{\frac{FV}{PV}} - 1 = z_2 \Rightarrow \sqrt[2]{\frac{100}{92.45}} - 1 \Rightarrow z_2 = 4.003\%$$

The important thing to notice is that the "real" present value of a cash flow received at t_2 is not only influenced by the two-year coupon rate, but also by the one-year rate. And the reason why the presented method to calculate zero rates out of a given coupon rate curve is called bootstrapping is that in the next step, we are going to use the one-year and two-year rates to calculate the three-year zero rate.

Let's think of a cash flow of €100 to be received at t_3 this time. The three-year coupon rate is 4.07%, so that the initial loan amount can be calculated as follows:

$$\frac{100}{104.07\%} = \frac{100}{1.0407} = 96.09$$

At t_3, the total payment obligation out of the loan will be €100 (€96.09 repayments plus €3.91 interest) and could be completely offset by the cash flow that is received at that time. But again, the loan requires annual coupon payments, so that the interest payment of 3.91 has to be fulfilled also at t_1 and t_2. We already know a way to neutralise these interim payments: we have to invest money at t_0. However, we have to invest two different amounts separately, as we need to neutralise two independent payments in this case.

Basically, there are two ways to do this but according to the no-arbitrage principle, both give us the same result. So let's try to prove this!

Alternative I:

This approach starts with neutralising the payment at t_2. We know that we have to invest enough money to create incoming payments of €3.91 to neutralise the coupon payment on the loan. As the two-year coupon rate is at 4%, we have to invest 3.91/1.04 = €3.76 at t_0 for two years. In a second step, we can neutralise the interim payments at t_1. The first thing we have to do is to calculate the total cash flow that has to be neutralised. We can't just use the value of €3.91 because there will also be a coupon payment out of our 2y investment at t_1:

−€3.91	Coupon to be paid for loan
+€0.15	Coupon to be received for 2y investment (€3.76 at 4%)
−€3.76	Total cash flow at t_1

In order to neutralise the total cash flow at t_1, we have to invest €3.62 at a rate of 3.98%. The present value of €100 to be received in three years therefore is: 96.09 − 3.76 − 3.62 = 88.71.

Alternative II:

In this case, it does not matter which cash flow is neutralised first. The investments that are required to neutralise the interim cash flows of the loan are done using zero-coupon instruments. This way they will not cause further coupon payments which also have to be neutralised.

The first step is very easy: we have to invest €3.76 for one year in a zero-coupon instrument with a zero rate of 3.98% in order to generate an incoming payment of €3.91 at t_1. The second step seems to be slightly more complicated – but not for us, as we have Equation 8 in our toolbox:

$$FV = PV * (1 + z_n)^n \Rightarrow PV = \frac{FV}{(1 + z_n)^n}$$

In the present case:

$$PV = \frac{3.91}{(1 + z_2)^2} = \frac{3.91}{1.04003^2} = 3.62$$

The present value of €100 to be received in 3y calculated using this alternative approach therefore is: 96.09 – 3.76 – 3.62 = 88.71.

The missing step is to use the calculated present value and the future value for the calculation of the 3y zero rate:

$$\sqrt[3]{\frac{FV}{PV}} - 1 = z_3 \Rightarrow \sqrt[3]{\frac{100}{88.71}} - 1 \Rightarrow z_3 = 4.074\%$$

The subsequent zero rates can be calculated using the same principles. This is very nice because we will be able to understand what's going on. But on the other hand, this can become really complex if you bear in mind that, nowadays, we have to deal with maturities up to 50 years. And that's why it was a big relief for me to find out that we can also use the following formula:

Equation 10

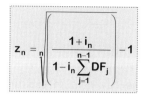

$$z_n = \sqrt[n]{\left(\frac{1+i_n}{1-i_n\sum_{j=1}^{n-1}DF_j}\right)} - 1$$

where: i_n = Coupon rate for n years
        DF_j = Discount factor for j years

The only thing we need to apply this formula to calculate zero rates from a given coupon curve successfully is Excel and a rough idea about what a discount factor is[19].

To calculate the present value of a future cash flow is also called discounting. A discount factor is simply the number with which a future cash flow must be multiplied in order to obtain the present value and could therefore also be interpreted as the present value of a future cash flow with the amount of one currency unit. Based on that, we can say that a discount factor can be calculated as follows:

Equation 11

$$DF_n = \frac{1}{(1+z_n)^n}$$

---

[19] And for those who will use the formula right now in a spreadsheet to recalculate the zero rates for two and three years, please do not send me an email to report a mistake in my calculations. But you are right: the real zero rates will be slightly different as Excel will not round to two decimals to maintain clarity. The good news: you will all be able to proof your skills at the end of this chapter.

4.2.2 The "Real" Bond Price

As we have seen in Section 3.2, the bond market does not use zero rates in order to discount the stream of cash flows within the pricing process. In fact, all cash flows are discounted using a constant coupon rate: the yield to maturity. This is obviously inaccurate and we now want to examine the deviation in prices using the two different approaches.

Let's use our previous five-year EUR government bond with a coupon of 4.12% for that. We calculated the bond price for a yield to maturity of 3.35% in Section 3.2.2 and the result was 103.49 using the bond pricing formula. If we want to calculate the theoretically correct bond price, we have to use zero rates to discount the single cash flows. The following table shows the EUR government rate curve and the derived[20] zero rates for the particular maturities:

Maturity in years	Coupon rate	Zero rate
1	3.23%	3.230000%
2	3.25%	3.250325%
3	3.27%	3.270879%
4	3.32%	3.323219%
5	3.35%	3.354682%

Using these zero rates, the bond price is calculated as follows:

$$P = \frac{4.12}{(1+3.23\%)^1} + \frac{4.12}{(1+3.250325\%)^2} + \frac{4.12}{(1+3.270879\%)^3}$$
$$+ \frac{4.12}{(1+3.323219\%)^4} + \frac{104.12}{(1+3.354682\%)^5}$$

$$P = 103.50$$

---

[20] The rates are calculated within a spreadsheet using Equation 10.

The price difference between the two pricing models is only marginal (0.01). So were we a bit overhasty in criticising the bond market participants for being inaccurate?

Remember, we said that there are two assumptions in the bond price formula that will lead to inaccurate results: the reinvestment assumption and the assumption of a flat yield curve. Well, if you have a closer look at the given coupon curve, you will find that it's not very steep – the difference between one-year and five-year coupon rates is just 12 basis points. That is to say that in this case, the assumption of a flat yield curve is not too far from reality. But what if we change the shape of the curve as follows?

Maturity in years	Coupon rate	Zero rate
1	2.00%	2.000000%
2	2.22%	2.222447%
3	2.60%	2.611950%
4	2.99%	3.018437%
5	3.35%	3.401110%

The "real" present value of the bond cash flow will go up to 103.54 whereas the result using the bond price formula will remain unchanged, as the yield to maturity has not changed at all. In other words: the steeper the curve, the larger the deviation between the market price of the bond and the sum of the accurate present values of its cash flows. That still does not convince the bond market participants to adjust their pricing approach but in the derivative markets, people are aware of that and therefore use zero rates to calculate the present value of cash flows and to price various financial instruments.

4.3 Forward Rates

A forward rate could generally be defined as an interest rate for a future period of time, e.g. for a five-year investment starting in one year from now. Within the group of forward rates, we can then differentiate the forward coupon rates and the forward zero rates. The forward coupon rate determines the interest rate on a coupon paying instrument with a forward start, the forward zero rate is the implied annualised yield on a forward starting zero-coupon instrument. And as we have seen in the previous section, these two rates are generally not identical.

4.3.1 Money Market Forwards

But how do we obtain these forward rates? If we work in the loan department of a bank and one of our clients needs to borrow money for six months starting in six months, how will we fix the price, i.e. the rate? The first thing we can do is to make a forecast of where six-month rates are going to be in six months' time and use this expectation to fix the price. Let's say that the current six-month rate is at 4%. We expect a slight increase in rates over the next six months due to inflation pressures so that our forecast for six-month rates in six months is 4.20%. In other words: we expect to be able to borrow the money we have to lend to the client in six months at a rate of 4.20%. But should we really charge 4.20% to the client? Of course not! The main reason for the bank to pay our salary is that they expect us to make some profits – so we definitely should add a margin. But simply adding a margin won't be enough because in many cases, our employer does not want us to create interest rate risk. And that's exactly what we would do by using our expectations for pricing the loan. Although we are all experts, there is still a small chance that our forecast turns out to be wrong. And imagine the mood of our boss in a scenario where six-month rates in six months are higher than initially expected and the bank has to pay 4.40% for its funding. As we lent the money to the client at a rate of 4.20% plus a margin, this would mean that the margin has decreased by 20 basis points due to unexpected interest rate developments.

We have to find a way to eliminate this interest rate risk and this is quite simple: we just need to fix our funding costs today. In order to lock in the costs for a six-month borrowing starting in six months from now, we simply have to borrow money for 12 months today and invest the money for the first six months:

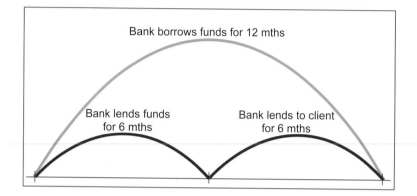

The interest rate for six months starting in six months (or simply: 6M6M forward) depends on the current 6M and 12M rate. Given the two rates below, how can we calculate the exact forward rate we should charge to the client?

Maturity	Interest rate
6M	4.00%
12M	4.30%

As previously announced, we will now come back to the no-arbitrage principle. The basic idea is that the future value of the following two investment alternatives must be the same:

Alternative I:

Invest money today for 12M at the current rate. The future value of €1 could be simply calculated as follows[21]:

$$FV = PV + \text{Coupon payment} = PV + (PV * 12M \text{ coupon} * DCF)$$

$$\Rightarrow PV * (1 + 12M \text{ coupon} * DCF)$$

$$\Rightarrow 1 * \left(1 + 4.3\% * \frac{365}{360}\right) = 1.0436$$

Alternative II:

Invest money today for 6M at the current rate and reinvest the payment that is received after 6M for the subsequent 6M at the current 6M6M forward rate. The future value in this case could be calculated as follows:

$$FV = PV + \text{Coupon on 6M investment} + \text{Coupon on reinvestment(6M6M)}$$

$$\Rightarrow [PV + (PV * 6M \text{ coupon} * DCF)] * (1 + 6M6M \text{ coupon} * DCF)$$

$$\Rightarrow [PV * (1 + 6M \text{ coupon} * DCF)] * (1 + 6M6M \text{ coupon} * DCF)$$

$$\Rightarrow \left[1 * \left(1 + 4\% * \frac{181}{360}\right)\right] * \left(1 + 6M6M \text{ coupon} * \frac{184}{360}\right)$$

According to the no-arbitrage principle, one can say:

$$\left(1 + 4.3\% * \frac{365}{360}\right) = \left(1 + 4\% * \frac{181}{360}\right) * \left(1 + 6M6M \text{ coupon} * \frac{184}{360}\right)$$

$$\Rightarrow \frac{\left(1 + 4.3\% * \frac{365}{360}\right)}{\left(1 + 4\% * \frac{181}{360}\right)} = \left(1 + 6M6M \text{ coupon} * \frac{184}{360}\right)$$

---

[21] We do not use the classic future value formula here, as both rates that are involved to calculate the forward have a maturity not exceeding one year. That is to say that there will only be one coupon payment each which takes place at maturity. To be more accurate, we then can use the real coupon payments which can be worked out as shown in Chapter 2. The day count convention we are using here is ACT/360 and the number of days should be 181 for 6M and 365 for 12M.

$$\Rightarrow \left[\frac{\left(1 + 4.3\% * \frac{365}{360}\right)}{\left(1 + 4\% * \frac{181}{360}\right)} - 1 \right] = \text{6M6M coupon} * \frac{184}{360}$$

$$\Rightarrow \left[\frac{\left(1 + 4.3\% * \frac{365}{360}\right)}{\left(1 + 4\% * \frac{181}{360}\right)} - 1 \right] * \frac{360}{184} = \text{6M6M coupon} = 4.5045\%$$

The interest rate we should charge the client for the 6M6M period is approximately 4.50% (plus the aimed margin), as this is the cost of borrowing we could lock in today using the current interest rates.

The calculation above could be condensed to the following formula:

Equation 12

$$r_{fwd} = \left[\frac{\left(1 + \frac{r_l * d_l}{\text{Basis}}\right)}{\left(1 + \frac{r_s * d_s}{\text{Basis}}\right)} - 1 \right] * \frac{\text{Basis}}{d_l - d_s}$$

where: r   = Interest rate

d   = Number of days of period

s   = Short period

l   = Long period

Unfortunately, this formula could only be used if the following conditions are met:

1. Neither the short nor the long period are allowed to exceed a term of one year.

2. The interest rates that are used must be quoted as per annum rates or zero rates (both rates are identical if Condition 1 is fulfilled).

4.3.2 Capital Market Forwards

What if we want to invest money for more than a year with a forward start? How can we work out the rate we should demand in this case? It's a pity that we cannot use Equation 12 but at least, there is some good news: the principles to be applied here are exactly the same.

Let's assume we want to invest €100 for two years starting in three years' time and receive an annual coupon payment. What is a fair rate we should receive for our investment? Let's take the steeper yield curve used in Section 4.2.2 as an example this time:

Maturity in years	Coupon rate
1	2.00%
2	2.22%
3	2.60%
4	2.99%
5	3.35%

All we now have to do is to calculate the 3y2y coupon rate (the two-year rate three years forward). And as we already said, the principles we have to use for this calculation are the same. So instead of investing the money on a forward basis, we can invest it today for the full five years and then borrow the amount back for the first three years, as we might not have the money yet. According to the no-arbitrage principle, both alternatives must give us the same return. In other words, we simply have to solve the following equation in order to calculate the 3y2y coupon rate:

$$PV * (1 + 3y\ coupon)^3 * (1 + 3y2y\ coupon)^2 = PV * (1 + 5y\ coupon)^5$$

Or is this wrong? Of course it is! The equation above contains the classic future value formula (Equation 5) and as we have already mentioned a couple of times, the results will only be correct if the applied interest rates are zero rates. If we will use the given coupon rates to calculate the 3y2y coupon rate, the result will be horribly wrong, as we will ignore the fact that interim coupon payments have to be reinvested:

Year	0	1	2	3	4	5
Cash flow of 5y coupon investment	−100	3.35	3.35	3.35	3.35	103.35
Cash flow of 3y coupon funding	100	−2.60	−2.60	−102.60		

As we can see, the interim payments of the two examined coupon investments do not match so that there will be reinvestment risk on the remaining amounts. Sure, in theory, we are able to neutralise these remainders step by step and therewith eliminate the reinvestment problem – but why should we do all this work if we have interest rates on hand where the reinvestment risk has already been removed? In practice, we simply use zero rates in forming our no-arbitrage equation:

$$PV * (1 + z_3)^3 * (1 + {}_3z_2)^2 = PV * (1 + z_5)^5 \Rightarrow \frac{PV * (1 + z_5)^5}{PV * (1 + z_3)^3} = (1 + {}_3z_2)^2$$

$$\Rightarrow \sqrt[2]{\frac{(1 + z_5)^5}{(1 + z_3)^3}} - 1 = {}_3z_2$$

We have learned how to calculate zero rates out of a given coupon rate curve in Section 4.2.1 and if we use Equation 10, we will get the following results:

Maturity in years	Zero rate
1	2.000000%
2	2.222447%
3	2.611950%
4	3.018437%
5	3.401110%

$_3z_2$ (i.e. the 2y zero rate 3y forward) therefore is:

$$\sqrt[2]{\frac{(1+3.401110\%)^5}{(1+2.611950)^3}} - 1 = 4.596245\%$$

This interrelationship could be condensed to the following formula:

Equation 13

$$_xz_y = \sqrt[y]{\frac{(1+z_{(x+y)})^{(x+y)}}{(1+z_x)^x}} - 1$$

where: $_xz_y$ = The y year zero rate starting in x years from now

Unfortunately, the use of zero rates in our equation has a disadvantage: the result is also a zero rate. Consequently, we have to transform this zero rate to a coupon rate before we are able to compare it with the rate our bank offers. This is something new, because we have only done it the other way round so far when we talked about bootstrapping. How can we calculate $_3i_2$ (i.e. the 2y coupon rate 3y forward)?

Well, as usual, we can use the no-arbitrage principle as a starting point: two investment alternatives with an identical risk profile must have the same return. So let's identify the two alternative investments:

Alternative I:

This alternative is given by a simple investment in a two-year zero-coupon instrument on a three-year forward basis. The forward rate for this instrument was calculated with 4.596245%, so the final payment in 5y for every €100 invested will be:

$$FV = 100 * (1 + 4.596245\%)^2 = 109.403745$$

Alternative II:

The second alternative is based on a 2y coupon investment, starting three years forward. But as the vigilant reader has already noticed, this coupon investment will cause an interim payment after Year 1 of its life cycle. This will then lead to reinvestment risk and to the fact that Alternative I and Alternative II are not directly comparable as the risk profile is not identical (there is no reinvestment risk embedded in Alternative I). So if we want to use the no-arbitrage principle, we have to eliminate the reinvestment risk first.

Until now, we have always eliminated the reinvestment risk by neutralising the interim cash flow using investments or loans at t_0. But there is a second way to do it: we could remove the uncertainty of our reinvestment using forward rates. For a better understanding, let's have a look at the cash flows of the 2y coupon investment starting in three years from now:

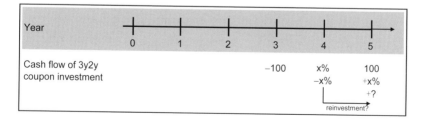

If the coupon of the 3y2y investment is known, we can eliminate the reinvestment risk by locking in the reinvestment rate via forwards today. The forward rate we have to consider in this case is the 4y1y rate (i.e. the one-year rate four years forward). As this rate has an investment period of one year and a coupon period of one year, it is again correct to say that the zero rate equals the coupon rate in this case. In this case, we therefore can use Equation 13 to work out the forward rate:

$$_4z_1 = \sqrt[1]{\frac{(1+z_5)^5}{(1+z_4)^4}} - 1 = \frac{(1+3.401110\%)^5}{(1+3.018437\%)^4} - 1 = 4.946070\%$$

We now know the reinvestment rate for the interim coupon payment so that the previous figure could be amended as follows:

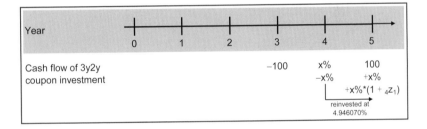

The interest on interest is no longer depending on future interest rate developments, i.e. the reinvestment risk is eliminated. We finally can compare both investment alternatives directly and use the no-arbitrage principle to derive the 2y coupon rate 3y forward:

FV Alternative I = FV Alternative II

$$\Rightarrow 100 * (1+_3z_2)^2 = PV + Coupon\ I + Coupon\ II$$
$$+ Return\ on\ reinvestment\ of\ Coupon\ I$$

$$\Rightarrow 100 * (1+_3z_2)^2 = 100 + (100 *\ _3i_2) + (100 *\ _3i_2) + (100 *\ _3i_2 *\ _4z_1)$$

$$\Rightarrow 100 * (1+_3z_2)^2 - 100 = (100 *\ _3i_2) * (1 + 1 + 1 *\ _4z_1)$$

$$\Rightarrow \frac{100 * \left(1 +_3 z_2\right)^2 - 100}{\left(1 + 1 + 1^* {}_4 z_1\right) * 100} =_3 i_2$$

$$\Rightarrow \frac{100 * \left(1 + 4.596245\%\right)^2 - 100}{\left(1 + 1 + 1 * 4.946070\%\right) * 100} =_3 i_2$$

The 2y coupon rate 3y forward is 4.588400% and therefore almost 1 basis point lower than the zero rate.

Well, the presented approach clearly is appropriate to show the concept behind forward rate calculation but quite frankly, if you want to calculate a 30-year coupon rate 20 years forward, the calculations might eventually get a little bit complex. In that case, you would have to deal with 29 interim cash flows and therefore you would have to calculate 29 forward rates and the respective reinvestment returns. As long as you do not make a mistake in setting up your spreadsheet, the result will be correct, but maybe the following equation can save some of your time:

Equation 14

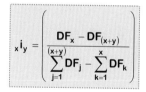

$$_x i_y = \left(\frac{DF_x - DF_{(x+y)}}{\sum_{j=1}^{(x+y)} DF_j - \sum_{k=1}^{x} DF_k} \right)$$

where: $_x i_y$ = The y year coupon rate x years forward

For our example, the equation will look like this:

$$_3 i_2 = \left[\frac{DF_3 - DF_5}{\left(DF_1 + DF_2 + DF_3 + DF_4 + DF_5\right) - \left(DF_1 + DF_2 + DF_3\right)} \right] = 4.5884\%$$

4.3.3 Forward Rates vs. Market Expectations

As we have seen in the previous section, forward rates can be derived from the current yield curve. The calculation is based on the fact that it is possible to lock in an interest rate for a period in the future in borrowing and lending cash simultaneously but for different maturities. We could therefore describe forward rates as objectively derived from current market rates using no-arbitrage calculations.

In many textbooks, forward rates are put on a par with the market expectation concerning future developments in interest rates. Expectations are subjective estimates of where prices will be in the future and therefore do not necessarily reflect the objectively calculated forward rates – or do they?

A further example might help to clarify this. The yield curve is given as follows:

Maturity in years	Coupon rate	Zero rate
1	5.40%	5.400000%
2	4.80%	4.785685%
3	4.68%	4.665035%
4	4.72%	4.711585%
5	4.76%	4.757194%

Let's say we have to borrow money for one year in 12 months and our forecast is that on- year rates should stay stable for the year. In other words: we expect 1y rates to be unchanged at the moment where we have to take out the loan. As we do not expect our funding costs to increase above the current prices, we simply can sit and wait for the year to go by.

This approach is obviously suboptimal and there are two main reasons for this. First, we will be liable to interest rate risk if we do not hedge our future funding costs. What if the 1y rate against our forecast increases to 6%? Whilst it is a question of opinion whether every financial risk should be hedged, there is a second incontrovertible reason for the fact that doing nothing is not the best solution in this case.

If we have a closer look at the given yield curve, we will find that the shape is inverted: long-term rates are below short-term rates. This leads to an interesting result if we calculate the 1y1y rate (i.e. the one-year rate one year forward). The zero rates are already given so that we could simply use Equation 13 to calculate the required rate:

$$_1z_1 = \sqrt[1]{\frac{(1+z_2)^2}{(1+z_1)^1}} - 1 = \frac{(1.04785685)^2}{1.054} - 1 = 4.174950\%$$

As a result, we get an implied forward rate which is significantly below the rate we expect for a 1y maturity in one year. So instead of doing nothing, we should lock in the cheaper forward rate today. To do this, we have to borrow money for two years at a zero rate of 4.785685% and simultaneously invest it for the first 12 months. The return for the first year will be 5.40% and this clearly over-compensates the borrowing costs for the same period. The remaining overhang will also subsidise the borrowing costs for the second period so that the total cost of funding will be below the two-year rate.

But what does this have to do with the relationship between forward rates and market expectations? Well, let's assume that we do need a lot of money. The amounts that we have to borrow and to invest in order to lock in a forward rate are so high that they will have an impact on the market rates. As soon as we start to borrow money for two years and invest it simultaneously for one year, the one-year rate will go down whereas the two-year rates will go up. And a closer look at the forward formula will show that this will lead to an increase in the forward rate, as the numerator will go up and the denominator will go down.

So in the first instance, forward rates are objectively derived from the current yield curve. But as soon as the deviation between these objectively derived rates and the expectation of the market gets too big, market participants will exploit these opportunities investing or borrowing money on a forward basis. This will then have an effect on the current shape of the yield curve which will finally lead to a change in forward rates. So to conclude, we can say that forward rates are not only objectively derived from the current yield curve but they also match the average market expectation.

However, we should not use these average market expectations as a forecast where interest rates will be in the future. The following graph compares the actual 10y EUR rate with the "market forecast" one year ago (i.e. the 10y rates one year forward, deferred by one year) and as we can see, the quality of this forecast is quite poor:[22]

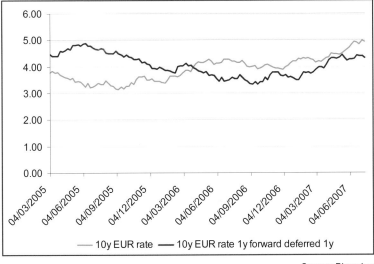

Source: Bloomberg

---

[22] To be fair, we have to add that this "forecast" just averages the expectations of all market participants. So we can't say that the whole capital market is not able to forecast future interest rates at least approximately right. It's simply that some are spot on and some are very wrong.

Exercises

1. Please calculate the zero-rate curve and the discount factors using the following coupon[23] curve:

Maturity in years	Coupon rate
1	0.91%
2	0.90%
3	0.97%
4	1.06%
5	1.16%
6	1.25%
7	1.35%
8	1.45%
9	1.55%
10	1.65%

2. Please calculate the one-year rates one year, two years and three years forward.

3. Please calculate the four-year zero rate six years forward.

4. Please calculate the four-year coupon rate six years forward.

5. If the ten-year coupon rate would be at 2.05%, how would the 1y9y coupon rate change in comparison to the initial scenario?

---

[23] Assume annually paid coupons and ignore day count conventions for simplification!

5

Interrelations and Characteristics

The only type of interest rate that is regularly directly observable in the markets is the coupon rate. In practice though, the other types of interest rates do play essential roles as well: zero rates are elementary building blocks for valuation and pricing processes, forward rates are frequently used by practitioners to spot interesting trading opportunities[24].

Based on the no-arbitrage principle, we developed a set of formulae in the previous chapter and this enables us to calculate every type of interest rate we need from a given coupon curve. If we illustrate our findings in a chart, it becomes apparent that there is a strong interrelationship between coupon, zero and forward rates:

---

[24] Traders often do not bet on current interest rates going up or down, they usually trade against a given forward rate.

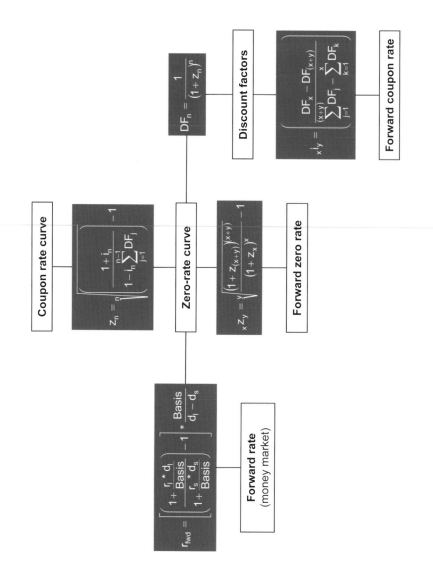

Discount factors

$$DF_n = \frac{1}{(1+z_n)^n}$$

Forward coupon rate

$$_x i_y = \frac{DF_x - DF_{(x+y)}}{\sum_{j=1}^{(x+y)} DF_j - \sum_{k=1}^{x} DF_k}$$

Coupon rate curve

$$z_n = \sqrt[n]{\frac{1+i_n}{1 - i_n \sum_{j=1}^{n-1} DF_j}} - 1$$

Zero-rate curve

Forward zero rate

$$_x z_y = \sqrt[y]{\frac{\left(1 + z_{(x+y)}\right)^{(x+y)}}{\left(1 + z_x\right)^x}} - 1$$

Forward rate
(money market)

$$r_{fwd} = \left[\left(\frac{1 + \frac{r_l * d_l}{Basis}}{1 + \frac{r_s * d_s}{Basis}}\right) - 1\right] * \frac{Basis}{d_l - d_s}$$

In practice, the workflow for calculating the required yields often looks as follows:

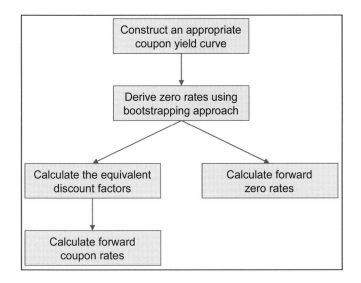

As all further calculations will be based on this set of coupon rates, great care has to be exercised in constructing the coupon rate curve. It is absolutely essential that every rate that is inserted matches the following criteria:

1. **Liquidity:**

    Is the underlying instrument traded regularly and in sufficient size?

2. **Credit risk:**

    Is the credit risk embedded in the underlying instrument comparable with the risk of the other instruments used? The issuer should be identical for all sampling points so that the curve will not be distorted due to different credit qualities.

Due to the functional link between the different types of interest rates, we can work out some interesting characteristics for forward rates. Let us have a closer look at a positively sloped, risk-free coupon curve for these purposes. As we have already learned in Chapter 1, there is more than one explanation for the shape of a yield curve. However, a positively sloped curve will always lead to forward rates being higher than the given coupon rates.

According to the no-arbitrage principle, there should be no difference in return between the following two investment alternatives:

1. Invest money for two years in a zero-coupon investment

2. Invest money for one year and use the 1y1y forward rate for reinvesting the lump sum plus the return after Year 1

$$\Rightarrow (1 + z_2)^2 = (1 + z_1) * (1 + 1y1y)$$

In other words: the 2y zero rate equals the time-weighted average of the current 1y rate and the 1y1y forward. In case of a positive yield curve, the 1y rate is below the 2y rate. In order to receive the same "averaged" return on Alternative 2, the implied 1y1y forward must be higher than the current one-year rate and also higher than the current 2y rate. So we can say that forward rates are above (below) the coupon rates when the yield curve is positively (negatively) sloped.

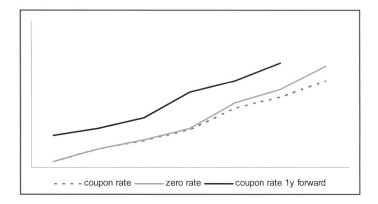

- - - - coupon rate ——— zero rate ———— coupon rate 1y forward

The coherence mentioned above also allows a further conclusion: forward rates are more volatile than the underlying coupon or zero rates. Let's take this zero-rate curve to prove this:

Maturity in years	Zero rate
1	5.30%
2	4.90%

The 1y1y forward rate can be calculated as follows (see Equation 13):

$$_1y_1 = \frac{(1+z_2)^2}{(1+z_1)^1} = \frac{(1+4.90\%)^2}{(1+5.30\%)} = 4.5015\%$$

Please note that the given curve was inverted so the forward rate is lower than the current 1y rate. But what will happen to the implied forward rate if we start to change the given zero rates?

First, we will shift the curve in parallel by 50 basis points and then recalculate the forward:

$$_1y_1 = \frac{(1+z_2)^2}{(1+z_1)^1} = \frac{(1+5.40\%)^2}{(1+5.80\%)} = 5.0015\%$$

The forward rate has also gone up by 50 basis points so we can say that a forward rate will mirror the parallel shift. This relationship does not come as a big surprise, as the difference between the two zero rates has not changed and we can easily derive from Equation 13 that the main influencing factor on the forward rate is exactly this difference. Thus, if we change the difference, we will therefore get very different results.

The 1y1y forward after an increase of 10 basis points in 1y rates and unchanged 2y rates:

$$_1y_1 = \frac{(1+z_2)^2}{(1+z_1)^1} = \frac{(1+4.90\%)^2}{(1+5.40\%)} = 4.4024\%$$

In this case, the spread between 1y and 2y zero rates has gone up by 10 basis points, the forward rate shows the same reaction as with the opposite sign.

The 1y1y forward rate after an increase of 10 basis points in 2y rates and constant 1y rates:

$$_1y_1 = \frac{(1+z_2)^2}{(1+z_1)^1} = \frac{(1+5.00\%)^2}{(1+5.30\%)} = 4.7009\%$$

In this case, the spread between one- and two-year zero rates has gone down by 10 basis points but the driving factor was the two-year rate this time. And as we can see, the forward rate has moved more than in the previous scenario. So the price reaction of a forward rate does not only depend on the spread to increase or decrease but also on which rate is responsible for this change. And if we refer back to the no-arbitrage explanation we used in the beginning of this chapter, this makes perfect sense: a one-year investment reinvested at the 1y1y forward rate must give us the same return as a two-year zero rate investment. If the one-year rate goes up and two-year rates stay constant, the reinvestment return has to go down in order to get the same "averaged" return for the whole investment horizon – but the change in rates will only affect a one-year period.

If the two-year rate goes up by 10 basis points, the return of the two-year zero-coupon investment will go up by roughly 0.2% (= $1.001^2 - 1$). As the one-year rate has not changed, the movement of the forward rate has to be bigger to keep the initial equation balanced. This shows the importance of calculating forward rates with as much accuracy as possible.

Solutions

Chapter 1

1. The yield on a bond consists of two building blocks: the risk-free rate and an issuer specific credit spread. This credit spread reflects the default risk and the expected severity of a default. For most countries, the default risk on a corporate bond should be higher than the one for government bonds, so investors will ask for a higher compensation (i.e. credit risk) for this type of investment. In many countries, government bonds are referred to as to be credit risk free.

    The spread is not only influenced by the issuer but also by the maturity of the underlying bond and normally increases with the duration of the investment. If we plot the credit spread for a specific issuer against the maturity, we will receive the credit curve which is normally positively sloped.

2. In the event of the insolvency of a company, there is a priority of claims on the assets of the company. The degree to which this actually happens depends on the legal environment of the country. A typical priority structure would be:

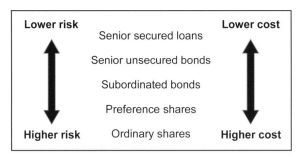

    So if the two bonds differ regarding the seniority, the default probability is identical but the expected loss severity might be different. Hence, there could be a difference in the credit spread.

Chapter 2

1.

1	Start date:	18.11.2007	Days: 15
	Maturity:	03.12.2007	Basis: 360
			Payment: 208,333.33
	Interest rate:	5%	
	Notional:	100 million	
	Day count:	ACT/360	

2	Start date:	01.03.2006	Days: 330
	Maturity:	31.01.2007	Y2: 2007, Y1: 2006
			M2: 1, M1: 3
	Interest rate:	4.5%	D2: 31, D1: 1
	Notional:	100 million	Basis: 360
	Day count:	30/360	Payment: 4,125,000

3	Start date:	01.02.2008	Days: 31
	Maturity:	03.03.2008	→ 2008: leap year
			Basis: 366
	Interest rate:	4%	Payment: 338,797.81
	Notional:	100 million	
	Day count:	ACT/ACT	

2. The equivalent rates can be calculated using this formula:

$$i_e = i_g * DCF_g / DCF_t$$

For Investment 2, we are given the following information:

i_g: 4%

DCF_g: 330/360

DCF_t: 336/360

$$i_e = 4.5\% * \left(\frac{330}{360}\right) / \frac{336}{360} = 4.5\% * \frac{330}{336} = 4.42\%$$

For Investment 3, we are given the following information:

i_g: 4.5%

DCF_g: 31/366

DCF_t: 31/360

$$i_e = 4\% * \left(\frac{31}{366}\right) / \frac{31}{360} = 4\% * \frac{360}{366} = 3.93\%$$

3. If the maturity of a coupon period falls on a Sunday, we need to know the business day convention, as these conventions define the procedure used to adjusting the end date of a coupon period or just the payment day in response to days that are not business days:

    Adjusted, modified following:
    The coupon period ends on Friday 29th January; the payment is made the same day.

    Unadjusted following:
    The coupon period ends on Sunday 31st January; the payment is made on Monday 1st February.

    Adjusted preceding:
    The coupon period ends on Friday 29th January; the payment is made the same day.

Chapter 3

1. $FV = PV * (1 + i\%)^n$

    $FV = 500 * (1 + 2\%)^{14} = 659.74$

2. $PV = \dfrac{FV}{(1 + i\%)^n}$

    $PV = \dfrac{1,000}{(1 + 4.2\%)^{10}} = 662.71$

3. $P = \displaystyle\sum_{t=1}^{n} \dfrac{C_t}{(1 + YTM)^t} + \dfrac{N}{(1 + YTM)^n} = \dfrac{4}{1.045^1} + \dfrac{4}{1.045^2} + \dfrac{104}{1.045^3} = 98.63$

4. As the yield to maturity is not given directly, we have to calculate it first:

    $\quad$ YTM $=$ Treasury yield (as risk-free rate) + Credit spread

    $\qquad\quad = 5.03\% + 0.25\%$

    $\qquad\quad = 5.28\%$

    Calculate the bond price using the YTM of 5.28%:

    $$\dfrac{7}{1.0528^1} + \dfrac{107}{1.0528^2} = 103.19$$

Chapter 4

1.

Maturity in years	Coupon rate	Zero rate	DF
1	0.9100%	0.9100%	0.990982
2	0.9000%	0.9000%	0.982241
3	0.9700%	0.9706%	0.971437
4	1.0600%	1.0620%	0.958625
5	1.1600%	1.1641%	0.943774
6	1.2500%	1.2566%	0.927814
7	1.3500%	1.3603%	0.909757
8	1.4500%	1.4650%	0.890165
9	1.5500%	1.5708%	0.869119
10	1.6500%	1.6780%	0.846705

2. The one-year rate for various forward starts is calculated using the following formula:

$$_x z_y = \sqrt[y]{\frac{\left(1 + z_{(x+y)}\right)^{(x+y)}}{\left(1 + z_x\right)^x}} - 1$$

One-year rate one year forward:

$$_1 z_1 = \sqrt[1]{\frac{\left(1 + z_2\right)^2}{\left(1 + z_1\right)^1}} - 1 = 0.8899\%$$

One-year rate two years forward:

$$_2z_1 = \sqrt[1]{\frac{(1+z_3)^3}{(1+z_2)^2}} - 1 = 1.1122\%$$

One-year rate three years forward:

$$_3z_1 = \sqrt[1]{\frac{(1+z_4)^4}{(1+z_3)^3}} - 1 = 1.3365\%$$

3. The same formula is used to calculate the four-year zero rate six years forward:

$$_6z_4 = \sqrt[4]{\frac{(1+z_{10})^{10}}{(1+z_6)^6}} - 1 = 2.3133\%$$

4. To calculate the four-year coupon rate six years forward, we have to use a different formula:

$$_6i_4 = \left(\frac{DF_6 - DF_{10}}{\sum_{j=1}^{10} DF_j - \sum_{k=1}^{6} DF_k} \right) = 2.3070\%$$

5. For the initial scenario, the nine-year rate one year forward is calculated as follows:

$$_1i_9 = \left(\frac{DF_1 - DF_{10}}{\sum_{j=1}^{10} DF_j - DF_1} \right) = 1.7384\%$$

To calculate the nine-year rate one year forward for the second scenario, we first have to recalculate the ten-year zero rate and the ten-year discount factor (as only the ten-year rate has changed, the rest of the curve will not be affected):

Maturity in years	Coupon rate	Zero rate	DF
10	2.0500%	2.1259%	0.810289

If we use the amended ten-year rate and the resulting discount factor to recalculate the nine-year coupon rate one year forward, the result will be 2.1867%.